D1072484

Dinosaurs Hatched!

by Ruth Owen

Consultant:
Dougal Dixon, Paleontologist
Member of the Society of Vertebrate Paleontology
United Kingdom

BEARPORT PUBLISHING

New York, New York

Credits

Cover, © Natural History Museum, London/Science Photo Library; 3, © Giedriius/Shutterstock; 4–5, © Natural History Museum, London/Science Photo Library; 6, © Sinclair Stammers/Getty Images; 7, © Franco Tempesta; 8, © Ruby Tuesday Books; 9, © James Kuether; 10–11, © James Kuether; 12, © Tim Boyle/Getty Images; 13, © James Kuether; 14, © Millard H. Sharp/Science Photo Library; 15, © Daniel Eskridge/Shutterstock; 16, Public Domain; 17, © Denis-Huot/Nature Picture Library; 18–19, © James Kuether; 20–21, © James Kuether; 22T, © Arth63/Shutterstock; 22B, © Puwadol Jaturawutthichai/Shutterstock; 23T, © wisawa222/Shutterstock; 23B, © Gorodenkoff/Shutterstock.

Publisher: Kenn Goin
Senior Editor: Joyce Tavolacci
Creative Director: Spencer Brinker
Image Researcher: Ruth Owen Books

Reader

Library of Congress Cataloging-in-Publication Data

Names: Owen, Ruth, 1967– author.
Title: Dinosaurs hatched! / by Ruth Owen.
Description: New York, New York : Bearport Publishing, [2019] | Series: The dino-sphere | Includes bibliographical references and index.
Identifiers: LCCN 2018049816 (print) | LCCN 2018053173 (ebook) | ISBN 9781642802504 (Ebook) | ISBN 9781642801811 (library)
Subjects: LCSH: Dinosaurs—Eggs—Juvenile literature.
Classification: LCC QE861.6.E35 (ebook) | LCC QE861.6.E35 O94 2019 (print) | DDC 567.9—dc23
LC record available at https://lccn.loc.gov/2018049816

For more information, write to Bearport Publishing Company, Inc., 45 West 21st Street, Suite 3B, New York, New York 10010. Printed in the United States of America.

10 9 8 7 6 5 4 3 2

Contents

A New Baby

Tap. Tap. Tap.

A baby animal is **hatching** from a big egg.

Is it a bird?

No! It's a baby dinosaur called a *Maiasaura*.

baby *Maiasaura* (mye-uh-SOR-uh)

A *Maiasaura* egg is almost as big as a football.

Dinosaur Eggs

All mother dinosaurs laid eggs.

How do we know this?

People found dinosaur egg **fossils**.

So how did the eggs become fossils?

fossil egg

rock

A dinosaur egg fossil is millions of years old!

a baby *Tyrannosaurus rex* inside its egg

Digging Nests

Millions of years ago, dinosaurs called *Saltasauruses* dug nests.

They chose sandy spots near rivers.

a *Saltasaurus* mother digging a nest

laying eggs

Each mother dinosaur laid 15 to 40 eggs in her nest.

Then she left the eggs to hatch.

Saltasaurus eggs in a nest

Saltasaurus mothers did not take care of their eggs or babies.

Saltasaurus (SALT-ah-sore-uhs)

Finding Fossils

After the eggs were laid, the river **flooded**.

The *Saltasaurus* eggs were buried in mud.

After a long time, the mud turned to rock.

Then in 1997, **scientists** found the eggs!

eggs

Each egg was round and about the size of a melon.

Turned to Rock

The scientists dug the eggs from the rock.

Using special tools, they looked inside the eggs.

a model of a baby *Saltasaurus* in its egg

They could see baby *Saltasaurus* dinosaurs!

The babies' bones had turned to rock.

An adult *Saltasaurus* was as long as two cars. It was nearly as heavy as an elephant.

13

Circle of Eggs

Other dinosaurs took care of their eggs.

A mother *Citipati* laid her eggs in a circle.

She sat in the middle so she didn't crush them.

Then she covered the eggs with her front legs.

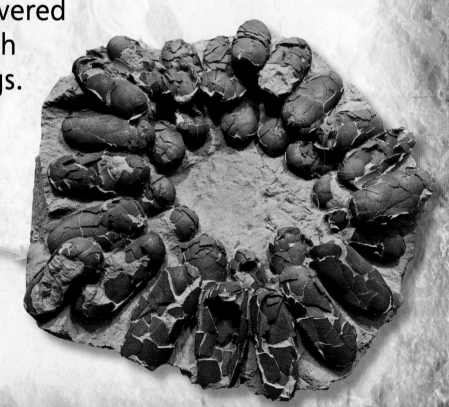

a circle of fossil eggs

A *Citipati* looked like a giant bird. It was as tall as a grown man.

Citipati
(SIT-i-pat-tee)

15

A Fossil Nest

One day, scientists found a strange fossil.

It was a *Citipati* sitting on eggs.

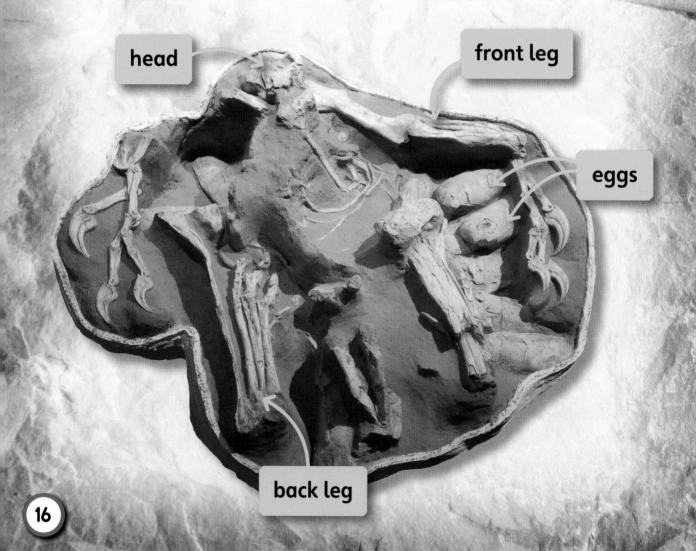

head

front leg

eggs

back leg

Was the *Citipati* keeping the eggs warm when it died?

Or was it keeping enemies away?

No one knows for sure.

father ostrich

Is the *Citipati* fossil a mom or dad? Scientists aren't certain. Today, some father birds sit on their eggs. Maybe some dinosaurs did this, too!

eggs

Good Mother

Maiasaura dinosaurs were good mothers.

First, a *Maiasaura* dug her nest in dirt or sand.

Then she laid up to 30 eggs in it.

She covered the eggs with plants to keep them warm.

Moms and Babies

When the baby dinosaurs hatched, they couldn't walk.

So the mother brought them plants to eat.

She watched over them until they were big and strong!

one-year-old *Maiasaura*

A baby *Maiasaura* was the size of a cat when it hatched.

newborn babies

Glossary

flooded (FLUHD-id)
covered by lots of
water from heavy rains
or overflowing rivers

fossils (FOSS-uhlz)
the rocky remains of
animals and plants
that lived millions
of years ago

hatching
(HACH-ing)
breaking out
of an egg

scientists
(SYE-uhn-tists)
people who study
nature and the world

Index

Read More

Bennett, Leonie. *Dinosaur Babies (I Love Reading: Dino World!).* New York: Bearport (2008).

Owen, Ruth. *Fossil Hunters at Work (The Dino-Sphere).* New York: Bearport (2019).

Learn More Online

To learn more about dinosaurs, visit
www.bearportpublishing.com/dinosphere

About the Author

Ruth Owen has been developing and writing children's books for more than ten years. She first discovered dinosaurs when she was four years old—and loves them as much today as she did then!